Aflame

ANCIENT WISDOM
ON MARRIAGE

compiled by

SAM & BETHANY
TORODE

WM. B. EERDMANS PUBLISHING COMPANY
GRAND RAPIDS, MICHIGAN / CAMBRIDGE, U.K.

Published 2005 by Wm. B. Eerdmans Publishing Co.
255 Jefferson Ave. SE, Grand Rapids, MI 49503 /
P.O. Box 163, Cambridge CB3 9PU U.K.

Printed in the United States of America

06 05 04 03 02 01   5 4 3 2 1

ISBN-10: 0-8028-2903-1
ISBN-13: 978-0-8028-2903-0

Quotations from *St. John Chrysostom on Marriage and Family Life*,
trans. Catharine P. Roth and David Anderson (pp. 26, 42, 46–47, 51,
55, 61, 63, 75–77, 81, 91, 95, 97, 100, 105, 113–14). Copyright © 1986 by
St. Vladimir's Seminary Press. Reprinted by permission of St.
Vladimir's Seminary Press, 575 Scarsdale Road, Crestwood, NY 10707,
www.svspress.com, 1-800-204-2665.

CONTENTS

Put me like a seal over your heart,
Like a seal on your arm.
For love is as strong as death,
. . . Its flashes are flashes of fire,
The very flame of the Lord.

SONG OF SONGS 8:6

PREFACE

MANY OF US have a vague notion of early Christianity as anti-woman and anti-sex. Recently, several popular books have asserted that the leaders of the ancient Church repressed the sensual spirituality of the "real Jesus."

There's a grain of truth in that. Some early theologians could tolerate sex only for the sake of procreation. And some monastic writers disparaged marriage, instead of praising both marriage and celibacy as complementary vocations.

That said, you don't need to go digging about for secret "lost Gospels" to read something good about sex from the early Christians. True Christianity has always upheld the beauty of the body and sexuality, the equal dignity of women, and the sanctity of marriage.

This shouldn't be surprising, since the Bible presents a remarkably positive vision for marriage and sexuality. In Genesis, God creates both men and women in His image and bids them to become "one flesh." The Song of Solomon celebrates sexual love. The Book of Proverbs encourages husbands to delight in their wives' bodies. In the New Testament, Jesus defends marriage as a divine institution. Paul calls it a "profound mystery" symbolizing the love of Christ and the Church. And the author of Hebrews says that the marriage bed—meaning sexual intercourse—is holy, and must be kept so.

In *Aflame*, we've gathered quotes that illuminate and expand on this biblical vision. Most are drawn from the first 400 years after Christ. Others come from ancient wedding liturgies and hymns, for which we don't know exact dates (likely, all were composed before AD 1000).

These ancient writings represent many diverse cultures—Greek, African, Middle Eastern, Roman, Celtic. Instead of clashing, their distinct tones blend together into one melody, like a marriage in which separate persons are united into a new whole.

9

As Ignatius of Antioch said, "When you are joined together in harmonious concord and love, Jesus Christ is sung. Taking up the song in unison, may you become a choir, singing to the Father with one voice, through Jesus Christ."

May the voices in this book draw us into that great choir, and may our lives and marriages become hymns of praise.

UNITY

In the Lord, neither is man independent of the woman, nor woman independent of the man.

1 CORINTHIANS 11:11

"For this reason a man will leave his father and mother and be united to his wife, and the two will become one flesh." This is a profound mystery, but I am speaking of Christ and the Church.

EPHESIANS 5:28–32

12

At the beginning God formed two creatures,
Adam and Eve; that is, man and wife.
He formed the woman from the man,
from the rib of Adam. He bade them both
to live in one body and one spirit.

AMBROSE OF MILAN

God created Adam and Eve that there
might be great love between them,
reflecting the mystery of divine unity.

THEOPHILUS OF ANTIOCH

14

From the beginning, God in His providence
has planned this union of man and woman,
and has spoken of the two as one: "male
and female He created them," and "there is
neither male nor female, for you are all one
in Christ Jesus." There is no relationship
between human beings so close as that of
husband and wife, if they are united as
they ought to be.

JOHN CHRYSOSTOM

Adam prophesied, saying "For this cause
a man shall leave his father and mother,
and shall cleave to his wife; and they two
shall be one flesh." This prophecy has its
fulfillment in ourselves. For he that marries
despises his family connection, becoming
one with his wife, fondly preferring her.
So much so that, for the sake of their wives,
some men submit even to death.

15

THEOPHILUS OF ANTIOCH

The virtue of man and woman is the same,
for the God of both is one. There is but one
Church, one chastity, one modesty.
Marriage is an equal yoke. Breath, sight,
hearing, knowledge, hope, obedience,
and love—all are one.

CLEMENT OF ALEXANDRIA

How beautiful is the marriage of two
Christians, two who are one in hope,
one in desire, one in the way of life they
follow, one in the religion they practice.

They are, in very truth, *two in one flesh*;
and where there is but one flesh there
is also but one spirit. They pray together,
they worship together, they fast together;
instructing one another, strengthening
one another.

TERTULLIAN

17

A man leaves his parents, who gave him life,
and is joined to his wife, and one flesh—
father, mother, and child—results from the
commingling of the two. The child is born
from the union of their seed, so the three
are one flesh. Our relationship to Christ
is similar; we become one flesh with Him
through communion, more truly one with
Him than our children are with us, because
this has been His plan from the beginning.

JOHN CHRYSOSTOM

A harmonious marriage alliance is at once
a holy love, an honorable love, and a
peace with God. God with His own lips
consecrated the course of this alliance, and
with His own hand he established the
coupling of human persons. He made two
abide in one flesh, so that He might
confer a love indivisible.

Paulinus of Nola

Husband and wife are not two, but one;
if he is the head and she is the body, how
can they be two? She was made from his
side; they are two halves of one organism.
God calls her a "helper" to demonstrate
their unity, and He honors the unity of
husband and wife above that of child and
parents. A father rejoices to see his son
or daughter marry; it is as if his child's
body is finally becoming complete.

JOHN CHRYSOSTOM

22

Love one another in the Lord, as being the images of God. Take care, husbands, that you love your wives as your own bodies. Wives, love your husbands, for you are one with them by virtue of your union.

IGNATIUS OF ANTIOCH

Marriage is the sacrament of love.

JOHN CHRYSOSTOM

24

If the two do not become one,
they cannot increase; they can increase
only by decreasing! How great is the
strength of unity! God's ingenuity in
the beginning divided one flesh into two;
but he wanted to show that it remained
one even after its division, so he made
it impossible for either half to procreate
without the other.

JOHN CHRYSOSTOM

By marriage, we are hands and ears and
feet to one another. And marriage has made
the weak one twice as strong, being a great
joy to friends and a sorrow to enemies.
And common worries lighten anxiety, while
joys had in common are sweeter for both.

GREGORY OF NAZIANZUS

25

Marriage is more than human.
It is a "microbasileia," a miniature kingdom,
which is the little house of the Lord.

CLEMENT OF ALEXANDRIA

When husband and wife are united
in marriage, they no longer seem like
something earthly, but rather like
the image of God himself.

JOHN CHRYSOSTOM

27

BEAUTY

Let the beauty of the Lord our God be upon us,
And establish the works of our hands for us.

PSALM 90:17

At your right hand stood the Queen,
   arrayed in vesture of gold.
Hearken, O daughter,
   and see and incline your ear.
And the King shall greatly
   desire your beauty;
For He is your Lord;
   you shall worship Him.

BYZANTINE WEDDING HYMN
Based on Psalm 45

30

Christ has adorned your souls with
perennial riches, and He has enriched both
of you with holy wedding gifts—hope,
devotion, fidelity, peace, chastity.

PAULINUS OF NOLA

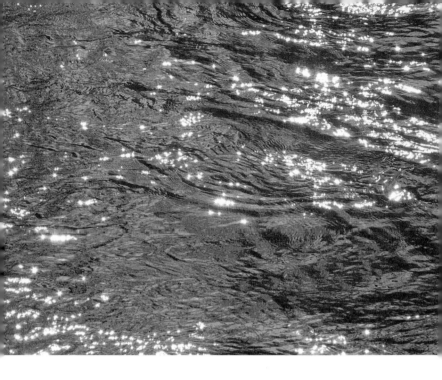

The souls of the good resemble fountains of the purest water. By their beauty, they allure passersby to drink of them—even those who are not thirsty.

Ignatius of Antioch

As for those women who radiate the beauty
of the soul, the longer time goes by and tests
their proper nobility, the warmer they make
their husband's love and the more they
strengthen their affection for him.

JOHN CHRYSOSTOM

33

It is the work a woman performs with her
own hands that creates true beauty.

CLEMENT OF ALEXANDRIA

"It came to pass," the Scripture says, "before he had finished speaking, Rebecca came out with her water jar upon her shoulder. The maiden was very fair to look upon, a virgin whom no man had known." Why does the Scripture tell us about the beauty of her body? To teach us the preeminence of her chastity, the beauty of her soul. Chastity is wonderful, and it is even more wonderful when it occurs together with physical beauty.

JOHN CHRYSOSTOM

"So Isaac took Rebecca, and she became
his wife, and he loved her." This story is
told to teach you the reasons for Isaac's
attraction and love, the good qualities
which his wife brought with her from her
home. Who would not have loved such a
woman, so virtuous, so beautiful, so
hospitable, generous, and kind, so brave
in her soul and vigorous in her body?

JOHN CHRYSOSTOM

35

By a ring power was given to Joseph in
Egypt; by a ring Daniel was glorified in the
land of Babylon; by a ring the uprightness of
Tamar was revealed; by a ring our heavenly
Father showed His bounty upon His son,
saying "Bring the fatted calf and kill it, and
let us eat and make merry."

Therefore, O Master, bless now this putting
on of rings with Your heavenly blessing.

Byzantine Wedding Liturgy

How many mysteries are hidden in the
splendor of the wedding rings!

Our Lord Jesus Christ who is betrothed to
the Church and who, through His blood,
has established a dowry for her, has forged
her a ring with the nails of His crucifixion.

SYRIAN WEDDING LITURGY

O Sons of Zion, arise, awake,
give the good news to the bride of light;
your Groom is risen and has conquered
    death by His power.
He will come to crown you with glory.
Go forth before Him covered with
    ornaments.
Sing a new song to Him that is risen,
    the fruit of life to them that are asleep.

ARMENIAN WEDDING HYMN

Now, as You blessed the wedding of our
forebears, bless, O Lord, the crowning of
these Your servants into marriage. For You
have given these Your children Your blessing
of sweetness, and You have placed upon
their heads a crown of precious gems.

Armenian Wedding Liturgy

Who can describe the love of God?
What man is able to tell of its excellent
beauty? Love exalts to unspeakable heights.
Love unites us to God.

CLEMENT OF ROME

Beauty on earth is not accidental, but sent to
us by the hand and will of God.

ATHENAGORAS

O beauty of the world! All things are
fashioned by the beautiful One.
O power and creativity of wisdom! . . .
He gave voices to the birds so that He
could receive sweet-voiced, heart-stirring
hymns in response to His own works.

XANTHIPPE

HARMONY

*Be filled with the spirit, speaking to one another
in psalms and hymns and spiritual songs, singing
and making melody in your heart to the Lord.*

*Submit to one another out of reverence for Christ.
Wives, submit to your husbands as to the Lord.
Husbands, love your wives, just as Christ loved
the Church and gave Himself up for her.*

EPHESIANS 5:18–19, 21–22, 25

44

Those that have been united together in
harmony by the Holy Spirit, like a harp,
are praising God continuously with Psalms
and praises and spiritual songs, day and
night, from the heart, without interruption.

COPTIC WEDDING LITURGY

When you are joined together in harmonious
concord and love, Jesus Christ is sung.
Taking up the song in unison, may you
become a choir, singing to the Father
with one voice, through Jesus Christ.

IGNATIUS OF ANTIOCH

46

Love your wife intensely, as Paul commands. For when he says, "Husbands, love your wives," he does not stop with this, but gives us a measure for love, "as Christ loves the Church." And how did Christ love the Church? "He gave Himself up for her."

JOHN CHRYSOSTOM

Let every man consider in what manner he
should be joined to his wife. He should have
delight in her and treat her with kindness.
Though he himself be naked, he must clothe
her. And she must regard him as her own
life. He must feed her, though he himself be
hungry; and give her to drink, though he be
thirsty. Likewise, it is her duty to serve him
in love and constancy in all circumstances.

Syrian Wedding Liturgy

Let us seek one thing in a wife: virtue
of soul and nobility of character, so that
we may enjoy tranquility, so that we may
luxuriate in harmony and lasting love.

JOHN CHRYSOSTOM

First, look for a husband who will really be
a husband and a protector. Don't look for
how much money a man has. Don't worry
about his nationality or his family's social
position. All these things are superfluous.
Look instead for piety, gentleness, wisdom,
and the fear of the Lord.

John Chrysostom

49

50

The human family is the primary and
essential element of society. Peace in society
will be a direct result of peace in the family;
order and harmony in the political realm
will be a direct result of order and
harmony in the home.

JOHN CHRYSOSTOM

Teach your wives to walk in the faith, tenderly loving their husbands in purity and truth, and to train up their children in the knowledge and fear of God.

Polycarp of Smyrna

52

Perform everything in harmony with Christ. Wives, be subject to your husbands in the fear of God. Children, obey your parents and love them affectionately, as co-workers with God in your birth. Husbands, love your wives, as fellow servants of God, as your own body, as companions in life, and as partners in the procreation of children.

IGNATIUS OF ANTIOCH

Husband and wife should both be in
harmony through good reasoning and love.
Neither of them should make decisions
separately without consulting with the
other. In this way their offspring may
be blessed.

Coptic Wedding Liturgy

When a wife is in harmony and peace with
her husband, nothing will be unpleasant,
even if innumerable storms arise every day.
When a woman is so decorous and chaste
and endowed with every virtue, she will
undoubtedly be able to attract her husband
and subject him to love for her. When she
has caught him, she will undoubtedly be
able to keep him willingly helping her in
the care of the children.

John Chrysostom

One's partner for life, the mother of one's children, the source of one's every joy, should never be fettered with fear and threats, but with love and patience. What kind of marriage can there be when the wife is afraid of her husband? What sort of satisfaction could a husband have if he lives with his wife as if she were a slave, and not with a woman by her own free will? Suffer anything for her sake, but never disgrace her, for Christ never did this with the Church.

JOHN CHRYSOSTOM

Do not be obstinate when your gentle
wife offers you her love. You are not a
master, but a husband. What you have
acquired is not a servant, but a wife.
God designed you to be a guide to her,
not a dictator. Share in her activities.
Share in her love.

Ambrose of Milan

57

Neither husband nor wife is his or her own master, but rather are each other's servants.

JOHN CHRYSOSTOM

For all the baptized there is the one task; both sexes must incorporate the perfect man, and Christ as all in all must be our common Head.

PAULINUS OF NOLA

May the Lord who began His divine
miracles at the wedding of Cana of Galilee,
bless you in your new life and bless your
house and transform things that create
division into means of blessing, and fill
your hearts with spiritual love.

COPTIC WEDDING LITURGY

JOY

As the bridegroom rejoices over the bride,
So your God will rejoice over you.

ISAIAH 62:5

Let us rejoice and be glad and give Him glory!
For the wedding of the Lamb has come,
and His bride has made herself ready.

REVELATION 19:7

Be exalted like Abraham, O bridegroom,
and be blessed like Isaac, and multiply like
Jacob, walking in peace and keeping God's
commandments in righteousness.

And you, O bride, be exalted like Sarah,
and be blessed like Rebecca, and multiply
like Rachel, and rejoice in your husband,
for this is well-pleasing to God.

Byzantine Wedding Liturgy

Our Lord, nourish with the riches of Your
grace these Your servants who are united
together, and make them joyful with
Your gift. Satisfy them with the perfection
of Your divine commandments, that they
may sing praises unto You with exceeding
joy, and be happy before You.

Syrian Wedding Liturgy

63

It is God who sows these loves in men
and women. He causes both those who give
their children in marriage and those who
marry great joy. Therefore Paul said,
"This is a great mystery."

JOHN CHRYSOSTOM

Bless this marriage, and grant to these
Your servants a peaceful life, length of days,
chastity, mutual love in the bond of peace,
long-lived offspring, gratitude from their
children, and a crown of glory that will not
fade away. Fill their house with wheat,
wine, oil, and every good thing, so that
they may give in turn to those in need.

BYZANTINE WEDDING LITURGY

The Heavenly Banquet

I would like to have the angels of Heaven
    in my own house;
with vats of good cheer
    laid out for them.

I would like to have the three Marys,
    their fame is so great.
I would like people
    from every corner of Heaven.

I would like them to be cheerful
    in their drinking.
I would like to have Jesus, too,
    here amongst them.

I would like a great lake of beer
    for the King of Kings.
I would like to be watching Heaven's family
    drinking it through all eternity.

BRIGID OF IRELAND

66

How can we ever adequately describe the
happiness of that marriage which the Church
arranges, the Sacrifice strengthens, upon
which the blessing sets a seal, at which
angels are present as witnesses, and to
which the Father gives His consent?

TERTULLIAN

O Lord, inflame these lovers with the fire
of love. In the morning of all their days,
may they awake unto joy!

SYRIAN MARRIAGE BLESSING

PURITY

Marriage should be honored by all,
and the marriage bed kept pure.

HEBREWS 13:4

72

The marriage that is consummated according
to the Word is certainly sanctified, if the
union be under subjection to God, and be
conducted with a true heart, in full assurance
of faith, having hearts sprinkled from an evil
conscience, and the body washed with pure
water, and holding the confession of hope;
for He is faithful that promised.

CLEMENT OF ALEXANDRIA

Blessed are You, O Lord our God,
priest of mystical and pure marriage,
creator of the law of marriage of the body,
preserver of immortality, and provider
of the good things in life.

BYZANTINE WEDDING LITURGY

74

Christ honored a marriage and, far from
being ashamed of it, adorned the occasion
with His presence and His gift. He brought
a greater wedding gift than any other, when
He changed the nature of water into wine.

JOHN CHRYSOSTOM

Through Your unutterable gift and manifold
goodness, You came to Cana of Galilee and
blessed the marriage there, to make manifest
that it is Your will that there should be lawful
marriage and procreation.

BYZANTINE WEDDING LITURGY

At Cana, Christ confirmed what
He instituted in Paradise.

AUGUSTINE OF HIPPO

You blessed the wedding in Cana of
Galilee, and showed Your divine glory to
Your disciples by changing the water into
wine, and did not despise marriage but
blessed it as a high-Priest and established it
with Your word, which cannot lie, saying:
"Therefore what God has joined together,
let no man separate."

ARMENIAN WEDDING LITURGY

O God who transformed water into wine by
Your divine power, bless Your two servants
and purify them with Your love for mankind.

COPTIC WEDDING LITURGY

Some reject marriage, teaching that it is not the appointment of God, and others abhor certain kinds of food. But we, who are the children of God and the sons of peace, say that every creature is good, and nothing abominable. Everything for the support of life, when partaken of righteously, is very good; for, according to Scripture, "all things were very good." We believe that lawful marriage and the begetting of children are honorable and undefiled.

THE APOSTOLIC CONSTITUTIONS

St. Paul does not despise physical unity, but
uses spiritual unity to illustrate it. How
foolish are those who belittle marriage! If
marriage were something to be condemned,
Paul would never call Christ a bridegroom
and the Church a bride.

79

JOHN CHRYSOSTOM

80

We honor marriage and call it blessed,
since God blessed it by joining together male
and female. Wise Solomon says, "A wife is
suited to her husband by the Lord." And
David says, "Your wife shall be as a fruitful
vine by the sides of your house; your children
like olive branches around your table."
Thus, marriage is honorable and comely,
and the begetting of children is pure.

THE APOSTOLIC CONSTITUTIONS

Truly, virginity by itself is nothing, nor
marriage, nor life as a monk, nor life in the
world. For God seeks the desire of a person,
and gives the Spirit to everyone.

MACARIUS OF EGYPT

Christ Himself was conceived in a pure
but human belly, and slipped out from
a woman's womb, thus mixing half
of human marriage with divinity.

GREGORY OF NAZIANZUS

The sexual union of man and wife, if it be
with righteousness, is pleasing to God.
"For the One that made them in the
beginning made them male and female;
and He blessed them, and said, 'Increase and
multiply, and fill the earth.'" If, therefore,
the difference of sexes was ordained by
God for the generation of mankind, then
the union of male and female must be
agreeable to his mind.

83

THE APOSTOLIC CONSTITUTIONS

As long as God forms man, we would be
guilty of audacity if we thought of the
generation of children as something offensive.
The Almighty Himself is not ashamed to
make use of it in working with His undefiled
hands; for He says to Jeremiah, "Before I
formed you in the womb I knew you."
And Job says to Him, "Your hands have
fashioned and made me."

Theophila

St. Paul tells us to seek peace and the
sanctification without which it is impossible
to see the Lord. So whether we presently
live in virginity, in our first marriage, or in
our second, let us pursue holiness, that we
may be accounted worthy to see Him
and attain the Kingdom of Heaven.

JOHN CHRYSOSTOM

DESIRE

I am my beloved's,
And his desire is for me.

Come, my beloved, let us go out into the country,
Let us spend the night in the villages.
Let us rise early and go to the vineyards;
Let us see whether the vine has budded
And its blossoms have opened,
And whether the pomegranates have bloomed.
There I will give you my love.

SONG OF SONGS 7:10–13

Then came this greatest marvel of the all-wise
Word: taking that man whom He'd formed . . .
by His great life-giving hand, He removed from
his side a sole rib, and built it into a woman,
and, mixing desire in their breasts, He set
them both loose to embrace each other.

Gregory of Nazianzus

How marvelous, indeed, is this institution
of God which fashioned the two sexes,
male and female! By the union of the two
sexes, through the excitement of pleasure,
a child is produced, lest the condition of
mortality cause the extinction of the
whole race of living beings.

LACTANTIUS

89

They come to be made into one body.
See the mystery of love! How do they
become one flesh? As if she were gold
receiving the purest of gold, the woman
receives the man's seed with rich pleasure,
and within her it is nourished, cherished,
and refined. It is mingled with her own
substance and then she returns it as a child!

But suppose there is no child; do they
then remain two and not one? No; their
intercourse effects the joining of their
bodies, and they are made one, just as
when perfume is mixed with ointment.

JOHN CHRYSOSTOM

Some of you call my words immodest,
because I speak of the nature of marriage.
By calling my words immodest, you condemn
God, who is the author of marriage.

JOHN CHRYSOSTOM

I could explain to you the marvelous
workings of the genitals, if modesty did not
constrain me. These matters ought to be
reverenced by us, and should be veiled with
reticence. Irreverent men commit the greatest
crime by profaning this divine and admirable
work of God, which was ordained by His
unfathomable design for the human race.

LACTANTIUS

93

And God cast Adam into a deep sleep and he slept.
What does the phrase "deep sleep" signify?
Does it not mean that when we contemplate
a conjugal union we seem to be turning our
eyes gradually in the direction of God's
kingdom? Do we not seem, as we enter into
a vision of this world, to partake a little
of things divine?

AMBROSE OF MILAN

The sleep of the first man prefigured the
embraces of nuptial love. . . . It is probably
for this reason that a man is said to leave
his father and mother, since he is unmindful
of all other things when united to his wife
in the embrace of love.

THEOPHILA

May the Lord, who has pleasure in the life of men, take delight in your life also and bless your union. May Christ, the heavenly bridegroom, seal your marriage with His own true seal. May you be happy in each other, as Christ delights in His Church. May the right hand of mercy come upon you, remain with you and defend you from all affliction.

SYRIAN WEDDING LITURGY

FRUITFULNESS

Your wife shall be like a fruitful vine
In the very heart of your house,
Your children like olive plants
All around your table.

Behold, thus shall the man be blessed
Who fears the Lord.

PSALM 128:3–6

The casting of seed into the furrows of the matrix is the beginning of the generation of children. Bone is taken from bone, and flesh from flesh, fashioned by an invisible power into another human being.

THEOPHILA

The child is a bridge connecting mother to father, so the three become one flesh, as when two cities divided by a river are joined by a bridge. And here that bridge is formed from the substance of each!

JOHN CHRYSOSTOM

101

A cornucopia full of fruits
    in all stages of development
resembles the course
    of human marriage;
it contains the old,
    young and middle-aged,
children who have already been born,
    and babies still unborn;
its fruits follow one another
    and appear
like the continuous succession
    of humankind.

EPHREM THE SYRIAN

The flowers of marriage are children,
which the Divine Husbandman plucks
from meadows of flesh.

CLEMENT OF ALEXANDRIA

Who gave the bones their fixed nature?
And who fashioned our arms and legs
with nerves, to be extended and relaxed at
the joints? Who prepared channels for our
blood, and a soft windpipe for our breath?
Only the Supreme Artist, making us to be
the rational and living image of Himself,
forming us like wax, in the womb,
from moist slight seed.

THEOPHILA

Place your confidence in God.
For He created you, and brought you into
existence, and formed you from a small,
moist substance—even from the least drop.

THEOPHILUS OF ANTIOCH

Everything should be secondary to us
compared to our concern for children, and
their upbringing in the teaching of the Lord.

JOHN CHRYSOSTOM

107

The things that parents teach their children
cannot have any weight unless they
themselves are the first to practice them.

LACTANTIUS

The creative power of God, pervading all things, is the real cause of the procreation of children, nurturing the seeds which are planted in the productive earth.

THEOPHILA

When a woman brings forth a child, her
swelling nipples are filled with sweet juices,
and her fruitful breast abounds
with a font of milk. Nothing else would be
fitting for a wise creature but to draw its
nourishment from the breast.

    LACTANTIUS

109

Now O Lord, bless these Your servants
to grow and multiply through your
compassion. Give them a blessed fruit, and
adjoin their faith with wisdom, purity, piety;
so they may unite through their bodies
and their souls.

COPTIC WEDDING LITURGY

Unite them in one mind, wed them into one flesh, granting them the fruit of the body and the procreation of fair children.

BYZANTINE WEDDING LITURGY

FIDELITY

So they are no longer two, but one flesh.
What therefore God has joined together
let no man separate.

MATTHEW 19:4–6

Let your fountain be blessed,
And rejoice in the wife of your youth.
As a loving hind and a graceful doe,
Let her breasts satisfy you at all times.
Be exhilarated always with her love.

PROVERBS 5:18

Husbands, love your wives, remembering
that at the creation, one woman was given
to one man—not several women to one man.

Wives, honor your husbands as your own
flesh. Be chaste, in fidelity to your husbands,
to whom you have been united according
to the will of God.

IGNATIUS OF ANTIOCH

It is love that asks, that seeks, that knocks,
that finds, and is faithful to what it finds.

AUGUSTINE OF HIPPO

Husband, say to your wife, "Our time here is brief and fleeting, but if we are pleasing to God, we can exchange this life for the Kingdom to come. Then we will be perfectly one both with Christ and each other, and our pleasure will know no bounds."

JOHN CHRYSOSTOM

If you desire a chaste wife, be chaste yourself.
Give to your wife what is due; take your
meals with her; spend time in her company;
read the Scriptures with her; do not grieve
her; do not quarrel with her; do not make
yourself hateful to her; furnish her with all
the good things you can; and, when you have
them not, make up for the lack with caresses.

117

The Clementine Homilies

Marriage is a sacred image,
and must be kept pure.

CLEMENT OF ALEXANDRIA

Keep yourself pure, as the habitation of God.
You are the temple of Christ. You are the
instrument of the Spirit.

IGNATIUS OF ANTIOCH

The faithful wife, when she devotes herself
to her husband, sincerely serves God.

CLEMENT OF ALEXANDRIA

Let him who has a wife seek nothing
further, but, content with her alone,
guard the mysteries of the marriage bed
chaste and undefiled.

LACTANTIUS

Guard your chastity, and don't allow thoughts
of another man's wife to enter your heart.
Always remember your own wife, and you
will never sin. Where purity dwells in a
righteous man's heart, iniquity cannot enter.

121

THE SHEPHERD OF HERMAS

Never call your wife by her name alone, but
with terms of endearment, honor, and love.
She won't desire praise from others if she
enjoys the praise that comes from you.
Prefer her before all others, both for her
beauty and her discernment, and praise her.

John Chrysostom

Cause their marriage to be honorable.
Preserve their bed blameless.
Mercifully grant that they may live
together in purity, and enable them to
reach a ripe old age, walking in Your
commandments with a pure heart.

BYZANTINE WEDDING LITURGY

SOURCES

AMBROSE OF MILAN (*c.* 339–97) is one of the four major Doctors of the Western Church. A powerful defender of orthodox belief, he fought Arianism (which denied the full divinity of Christ) and once publicly reprimanded the emperor for his part in a massacre.

THE APOSTOLIC CONSTITUTIONS (*c.* 380) is a manual of church doctrine and practice. It was compiled in Syria in the 4th century from earlier sources and attributed to the Apostles. In response to various gnostic heresies, it staunchly upholds the purity of marital love.

ATHENAGORAS (2nd century) was an early apologist. His *Plea for the Christians*, addressed to Emperor Marcus Aurelius, refuted false claims against Christianity.

AUGUSTINE OF HIPPO (354–430) was a convert from Neoplatonism who became one of the most influential theologians of the Western Church. He was born in North Africa and eventually became a bishop there. Though some of his writings seem unfortunately suspicious of sexuality, he defended marriage and procreation against the Manichaean heresy.

BRIGID OF IRELAND (*c.* 451–525) is the Patroness of Ireland. Many legends surround her life, but her friendship with Patrick is historically established. She founded two monasteries and a school of art renowned for its illuminated manuscripts. The whimsical and distinctively Irish poem, "The Heavenly Banquet," is traditionally attributed to her.

CLEMENT OF ALEXANDRIA (*c.* 150–215) was one of the greatest philosophers of the early Church. He was born in Greece but eventually settled in Alexandria, where he helped found the Alexandrian school of biblical interpretation, distinguished by its figurative, non-literal approach to Scripture.

CLEMENT OF ROME (1st century) was, according to tradition, the third Bishop of Rome and a martyr. His Letter to the Corinthians was written around the year 96.

THE CLEMENTINE HOMILIES (3rd century) is a collection of sermons purporting to be written by Clement of Rome, but more likely originating from later sources.

EPHREM THE SYRIAN (*c.* 306–73) was perhaps the greatest hymn-writer of the early Church. Over 400 of his hymns survive, covering various biblical and doctrinal subjects. His *Hymns on Paradise* explore the symbolism of the Genesis creation story.

GREGORY OF NAZIANZUS (329–89) was one of the three great "Cappadocian Fathers." Together with Basil and Gregory of Nyssa, he defended the orthodox view of the Trinity against Arianism. After serving as Bishop of Constantinople, he retired from public life and concentrated on poetry in his final years. His poem *In Praise of Virginity* upholds both marriage and celibacy as paths to holiness.

IGNATIUS OF ANTIOCH (*c.* 35–107) was martyred in the Roman Coliseum. As soldiers transported him to Rome from Antioch, where he was bishop, he wrote letters to several churches and individuals along the way.

127

JOHN CHRYSOSTOM (*c.* 347–407) is one of the most important theologians of the Eastern Church. As Bishop of Antioch, he earned the name "Golden Mouth" for his eloquent preaching. His homilies on Paul's letters are notable for extolling the beauty of marriage and sexuality. He was appointed Bishop of Constantinople, but was deposed when he refused to bend to the Empress Eudoxia. He died in exile.

LACTANTIUS (*c.* 240–320) was a renowned African-born rhetorician, hand-picked by Emperor Diocletian to teach at the court in Nicomedia. After converting to Christianity, he lost his position under Diocletian's oppressive policies. Then he turned his rhetorical skill to defending the faith. In his first book of apologetics, *The Workmanship of God*, he argued that the beautiful design of the human body points to the glory of its Creator.

MACARIUS OF EGYPT (*c.* 300–390) was one of the "Desert Fathers and Mothers," monastics who congregated in the Egyptian wilderness.

PAULINUS OF NOLA (*c.* 353–431) was one of many married priests in the early Church (later, celibacy became a prerequisite for priesthood in the Western Church). Paulinus and his wife, Therasia, embraced voluntary poverty and established a refuge for monastics and the poor in the French village of Nola. He was elected bishop after Therasia's death. In his poetry and letters, he celebrated marriage as a deeply spiritual union.

POLYCARP OF SMYRNA (*c.* 69–155) followed his friend and fellow bishop, Ignatius of Antioch, to martyrdom. One of his letters has survived, and also an eyewitness account of his last days.

THE SHEPHERD OF HERMAS (*c.* 150) records the visions and teachings of Hermas. In the 2nd and 3rd centuries, some churches included this book in the New Testament.

TERTULLIAN (*c.* 160–255) was an African convert to Christianity. He was married and wrote a beautiful tribute, *To His Wife*. Later in his career, preoccupied by thoughts of the end times, he exalted celibacy over marriage and fell into the rigorist heresy (believing that a person could not be forgiven of sin after baptism). Even so, *To His Wife* stands as one of the early Church's best statements on marriage.

THEOPHILA is one of the principal speakers in
The Banquet of the Ten Virgins, a Socratic-style
dialogue written by Methodius of Olympus,
Bishop of Lycia and a martyr (died *c.* 311).

THEOPHILUS OF ANTIOCH (2nd century) was a
bishop and apologist. His *Apology* argued for the
superiority of the Christian doctrine of creation
over pagan myths

XANTHIPPE appears in *The Acts of Xanthippe and
Polyxenia* (2nd century), which records the
exploits of two Christian women of uncertain
historicity.

BIBLIOGRAPHY

The Armenian, Byzantine, Coptic, and Syrian
wedding liturgies are in the public domain and
available on the Internet.*

Chrysostom, John, *St. John Chrysostom on
Marriage and Family Life*, trans. Catharine P.
Roth and David Anderson (Crestwood, NY: St.
Vladimir's Seminary Press, 1986).

Chryssavgis, John, *Love, Sexuality, and the
Sacrament of Marriage* (Brookline, MA: Holy
Cross Orthodox Press, 1996).

Ephrem the Syrian, *Hymns on Paradise*, trans.
Sebastian Brock (Crestwood, NY: St. Vladimir's
Seminary Press, 1990).

Evdokimov, Paul, *The Sacrament of Love* (Crestwood, NY: St. Vladimir's Seminary Press, 1985).

Gasparro, Giulia, Cesare Magazú, and Concetta Aloe Spada, eds. *The Human Couple in the Fathers*, trans. Thomas Halton, *Pauline Patristics Series* I (New York: Society of St. Paul, 1999).

Gregory of Nazianzus, *On God and Man: The Theological Poetry of St. Gregory of Nazianzus*, trans. Peter Gilbert (Crestwood, NY: St. Vladimir's Seminary Press, 2001).

Grube, George, ed. *What the Church Fathers Say About . . .* I (Minneapolis: Light and Life Publishing, 1996).

Lactantius, *Lactantius: The Minor Works*, trans. Mary Francis McDonald, *The Fathers of the Church* 54 (Washington, DC: The Catholic University Press, 1965).

O'Faolin, Sean, ed. *The Silver Branch: A Collection of the Best Old Irish Lyrics* (London: Jonathan Cape, 1938).

Roberts, Alexander, and James Donaldson, eds., *The Apostolic Fathers with Justin Martyr and Irenaeus*, *The Ante-Nicene Fathers* I (Grand Rapids: Wm. B. Eerdmans Publishing Company, repr. 1996).*

——, *Fathers of the Second Century*, *The Ante-Nicene Fathers* II (Grand Rapids: Wm. B. Eerdmans Publishing Company, repr. 1996).*

——, *The Fathers of the Third Century*, *The Ante-Nicene Fathers* VI (Grand Rapids: Wm. B. Eerdmans Publishing Company, repr. 1996).*

——, *Fathers of the Third and Fourth Centuries*, *The Ante-Nicene Fathers* VII (Grand Rapids: Wm. B. Eerdmans Publishing Company, repr. 1996).*

——, *Fathers of the Third and Fourth Centuries*, *The Ante-Nicene Fathers* VIII (Grand Rapids: Wm. B. Eerdmans Publishing Company, repr. 1996).*

——, *Recently Discovered Additions to Early Christian Literature*, *The Ante-Nicene Fathers* X (Grand Rapids: Wm. B. Eerdmans Publishing Company, repr. 1996).*

Tertullian, *Tertullian: Treatises on Marriage and Remarriage*, trans. William P. Le Saint, *Ancient Christian Writers: The Works of the Fathers in Translation* 13 (Westminster, MD: The Newman Press, 1951).

* *Translations adapted by the editors.*